Flash and Bang

Kaboom! The blast shatters the stillness and a red star-burst erupts in the night sky. A grand fireworks display never fails to delight young and old alike. Much of the magic of these spectacular *shells* lies in the way they so artfully combine sight and sound. Without the rumbling booms, ricocheting rat-a-tats, and whistling fizzles, the light show wouldn't be nearly as much fun. This is something the Chinese, who invented fireworks more than one thousand years ago, must certainly have realized. Their main purpose in creating such loud noises, however, was to chase away evil spirits from weddings, festivals, and religious ceremonies.

Today's fireworks pack a bigger punch than the paper and bamboo tubes that the Chinese launched in the past. But one thing about them has remained virtually unchanged. The explosive used to send them skyward and release their colorful *stars* is, and always has been, a powerful substance known throughout the world as gunpowder.

Gunpowder: Good or Evil?

An invention is a device or process designed by humans to solve a problem or meet a need. Gunpowder is less of an invention than a discovery. It wasn't devised for the gun. It came to light several hundred years before guns were even invented and was originally called powder.

When gunpowder was first identified, humans weren't quite sure how to put its flash and bang to use. Yet from the beginning, one thing was clear: its potential for destruction. Time and again, many of those who experimented with the explosive substance cautioned others not to tamper with it, even as they ignored their own warnings.

Over time, gunpowder would spark many inventions—some valuable, most violent. Rarely has a discovery impacted humanity so dramatically or divided it as deeply as gunpowder. The world's first explosive, and the only one available for nearly one thousand years, it came to be viewed as both miracle and monster.

Gunpowder made it possible for nations to grow and industrialize by giving people more control over the plan-

Inventions That Shaped the World

Gunpowder

TRUDI STRAIN TRUEIT

Franklin Watts
A Division of Scholastic Inc.
New York · Toronto · London · Auckland · Sydney
Mexico City · New Delhi · Hong Kong
Danbury, Connecticut

For Kyle, with love

The author would like to thank Robert Howard, retired curator of Industry and Technology at the Hagley Museum, for so kindly offering his insight. Also, special acknowledgment to Dr. Bert Hall, professor of history at the Institute for History and Philosophy of Science and Technology at the University of Toronto for sharing his expertise.

Photographs © 2005: Art Resource, NY/Erich Lessing: 47 (Kunsthistoriches Museum, Vienna, Austria), 45 (Universitaetsbibliothek, Goettingen, Germany); Bill Trueit: 80; Bridgeman Art Library International Ltd., London/New York: 61 (John William Hill/New-York Historical Society, New York, USA), chapter openers, 52 (R.S.A.F. Enfield Lock, Middlesex, UK), 54 (Trelleek/Private Collection/The Stapleton Collection); Corbis Images: 20 (Dave Bartruff), cover bottom right, 12, 14, 31, 48 (Bettmann), 7, 41 (Raymond Gehman), cover inset, chapter openers (Lowell Georgia), 15 (Christel Gerstenberg), 21 (Dallas & John Heaton/Free Agents Limited), 64 (Keystone View Company), cover bottom left (Gianni Dagli Orti), cover top left, back cover ghost, timeline bubbles (Bill Ross), 60 (Schenectady Museum; Hall of Electrical History Foundation), 24 (David Teniers II/Philadelphia Museum of Art); Fundamental Photos, New York/Jeff J. Daly: 22; Getty Images: 42 (Walker Evans/Time Life Pictures), 26, 30, 49 (Hulton Archive), 53 (Robert Laberge), 50 (MPI/Hulton Archive), 28, 32 (Time Life Pictures); North Wind Picture Archives: 19, 43, 56, 59; PhotoDisc via SODA: 69, timeline top border; Southern Pacific Company via SODA: 62; Superstock, Inc.: 35; The Image Works: 37 (HIP/The Board of Trustees of the Armouries), 63 (SSPL), 10 (Topham-HIP/Museum of London), 17 (Topham-HIP/The British Library); The Nobel Foundation: 66.

Cover design by The Design Lab
Book production by The Design Lab

Library of Congress Cataloging-in-Publication Data
Trueit, Trudi Strain.
 Gunpowder / Trudi Strain Trueit.
    p. cm. — (Inventions that shaped the world)
 Includes bibliographical references and index.
 ISBN 0-531-12371-5 (lib. bdg.)   0-531-16744-5 (pbk.)
 1. Gunpowder—Juvenile literature. I. Title. II. Series.
 TP272.T78 2005
 662'.26—dc22   2004030437

Contents

et's resources. It provided *civil engineers* with a more effi-
cient way to split rock, paving the way for building roads,
canals, tunnels, pipelines, and railroads. It offered a better
method of extracting the planet's minerals, stones, and
fuels. From ancient Chinese fireworks to submarine torpedoes, gunpowder proved its value as a *propellant.*

*Dynamite explodes and breaks open rock for an expansion of a gold mine in
Nevada.*

Along the way, this early rocket fuel boosted humans toward the first steps in space exploration.

Gunpowder has a dark side, too. Its discovery fueled a new military age, unleashing powerful guns and cannons never before seen on Earth. Its victims included those who manufactured it, the European knights whose armor it pierced, and the native tribes of the world whose bows and arrows were no match for it. Gunpowder has played a role in killing tens of millions of people.

Gunpowder may have altered the face of warfare on Earth, but it did not create it. Long before explosives, humans were fighting one another. Before gunpowder, battles were just as brutal, soldiers were just as fierce, and weapons were just as deadly.

Do Not Try This at Home

You should never attempt to make or handle gunpowder on your own. Gunpowder and other explosives are deadly materials. They should be made only by experts in the proper surroundings, where strict safety measures can be followed. Also, never pick up a gun or any type of deadly weapon, even just to look at without the direct supervision of an adult trained in the proper handling of firearms. You may unintentionally harm yourself or others.

Seeds of War

More than 2 million years ago, early humans reached for the earliest known weapons. In their quest to scare off large animals, and occasionally one another, these hunter-gatherers hurled whatever *ammunition* was handy, mainly sticks and stones. They also fashioned crude clubs from tree branches and stumps. Eventually, Paleolithic humans, who lived between 750,000 and 15,000 B.C., discovered the value of flint. Flint is a type of quartz rock that breaks easily into sharp pieces when struck. Old Stone Age people used these pieces as weapons or to cut and shape other types of weaponry. Over thousands of years, humans perfected their flint-sharpening skills, crafting the points of the first spears, swords, axes, and arrows.

About 8000 B.C, many hunter-gatherers began trading their *nomadic* ways for a more settled lifestyle. During the Neolithic Period (8000 to 5000 B.C.), some New Stone Age humans formed societies based on agriculture. They learned to grow crops, tend sheep and cattle, build shelters, and store food. The more people owned, however, the more they stood to lose. Bands of nomads frequently raided settlements, stealing livestock, food, and supplies. It also proved true that the more goods people had, the more they wanted. Villagers often attacked one another to

As early humans settled down in villages, they needed weapons, such as these daggers, to defend themselves and help prevent others from stealing their belongings.

secure the best farmland, herds, or water resources. Weapons became critical to survival.

The first civilizations, or societies, emerged in the Middle East. About 3500 B.C., cities began to spring up in the nations known today as Iraq, Iran, Syria, Egypt, and Turkey. With these new civilizations came the first religions, politics, organized militaries, and written languages.

The more "civilized" humans became, the more they fought. For more than two thousand years, the Sumerian city-states of Uruk, Kish, Lagash, and Ur, among others, feuded. Armed with spears and axes, Sumerians often headed into battle on chariots. They fought over politics,

Metal Mania

Discovered in Asia about 5000 B.C., copper was the first metal used to craft daggers, swords, and spear tips. People soon found, however, that copper was too soft to make effective weapons. It broke easily and couldn't keep a sharp edge. About 3500 B.C., the Sumerians developed bronze, a combination of copper and tin. Tin hardened the copper, and bronze weapons were able to hold both their shape and a sharp edge. The Sumerians heated the metal, then poured it into molds to cast bladed weapons and maces (a mace is a club with a spiked metal ball at one end). In 1600 B.C., the discovery of iron by the Hittites in present-day Turkey allowed them to make weapons tougher than bronze that could last a lifetime. In wet weather, however, iron had an irritating tendency to rust.

A phalanx of Macedonian soldiers marches into battle.

wealth, boundaries, and control of trade routes along the Tigris and Euphrates rivers.

Near the end of the eighth century B.C., Greek warriors introduced the first true military formation, known as the phalanx. Rows of foot soldiers advanced onto the battle-field in tight formation, their shields in front of them. The shields overlapped to provide maximum defense against flying stones, arrows, and iron-tipped javelins (light, short spears). On the battlefield, foot soldiers wearing metal body armor and helmets clashed with daggers, swords, and spears. Those on horseback or in chariots slung stones, threw javelins, and shot arrows.

Capable of firing its deadly missile several hundred yards or more, the bow was the ancient equivalent of the rifle. It was one of the most lethal weapons ever invented. First used in conflict about 16,000 B.C., early bows were made from flexible woods such as elm, ash, or yew. About 2500 B.C., archers in Egypt and Mesopotamia (present-day Iraq) invented the composite bow. Reinforcing a bow with a variety of materials, such as wood, horn, leather, and sinew (animal tissue), made it stronger and capable of sending its metal-tipped missile faster and farther. A well-crafted composite bow could fire a lightweight arrow up to .3 mile (0.5 kilometers)! In the fifth century B.C., the Chinese devised the crossbow, a bow mounted horizontally on a wooden frame. Not until the advent of firearms would humans possess another weapon as effective as the bow and arrow.

Look Out for Flying Objects!

Ancient cities needed to protect themselves from invading armies that sought the same things they were after: territory, resources, and power. Huge walls, sometimes 7 feet (2 meters) thick and 20 feet (6 m) high, were often erected around towns to keep enemies at bay. These physical barriers, called fortresses, were not enough to stop the most determined invaders.

To mount a *siege,* an army would cut off supplies to a fortified town to starve out its inhabitants. They also had to find a way under, over, or through defensive walls. This spawned the invention of siege engines, or war machines, most notably ballistae, catapults, and trebuchets. These types of heavy *artillery* were also used in battle.

Developed by the Chinese and perfected by the Greeks, a ballista (buh-LEE-stah) was a large crossbow mounted on wheels or on a stand. Some ballistae fired bolts, while others shot small stones. It required a crew of two to ten men to operate each machine. Bigger ballistae could shoot a 6-pound (2.7-kilogram) bolt 1,500

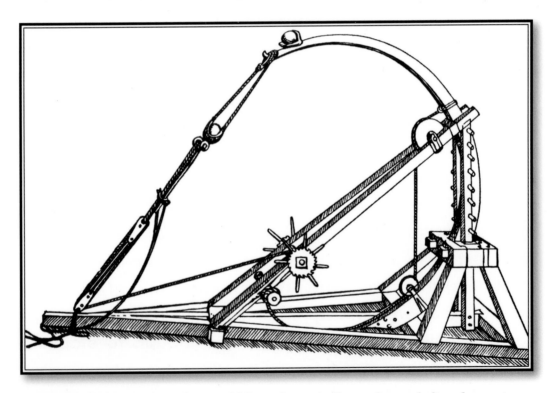

A ballista was a weapon that could launch a missile, such as a bolt or large stone, over a town's walls.

Wooden catapaults, such as this one, were used during the Middle Ages to launch stones at city walls or into enemy camps.

feet (458 m). A bolt shot from a ballista was so forceful that it could penetrate almost anything: metal armor, trees, and even more than one soldier.

A catapult was a giant wooden arm attached to a frame, with a sling, or pouch, at one end. It was used to lob stones at city walls or into enemy camps. A standard catapult could fling a 50-pound (23-kg) stone up to 1,500 yards (1,373 m).

Another type of catapult called the trebuchet (treb-ya-SHET) was a lever that used muscle power or gravity to fling its load. Initially, soldiers pulled on ropes to release the lever, but several centuries later the value of counterweights was discovered and soldiers let gravity do the work for them. Trebuchets could throw items too heavy for a typical catapult to handle and were far more accurate. Through the ages, armies used them to launch

Greek Fire: Inferno of Death

Invented in the Byzantine Empire (located in southeastern Europe and Turkey) in the seventh century, "Greek fire" was one of the most feared weapons of its day. The exact recipe for this flammable brew was a well-guarded secret, but historians believe it was most likely a concoction of petroleum oil, tar, turpentine, and sulfur (one of the ingredients in gun-powder). Once ignited, Greek fire could not be put out with water, a feature that made it perfect for sea battles. Pots of flaming Greek fire could be launched from a trebuchet or shot with an arrow from the deck of a ship. More often, this liquid fire was pumped through tubes and sprayed at the enemy. The fiery substance stuck to anything it touched—wood, sails, clothes, and skin—burning entire ships. It is rumored that only stale urine or vinegar could extinguish the raging inferno. It was such a devas-tating weapon that many governments and religious groups condemned its use. By the thirteenth century, the formula for Greek fire had been lost.

A trebuchet was a type of catapault that used muscle power or gravity to launch its missiles. In this depiction, the attackers have fired stones at the city walls and the defenders fight back by throwing smaller stones at the attackers.

an assortment of awful things: 300-pound (136-kg) stones, firebombs, bees' nests, bags of snakes, the heads of enemy prisoners, dead horses, and victims of the bubonic plague (to spread the disease). During a siege, soldiers used battering rams and crow bars to smash gates, catapults and trebuchets to shatter walls, and scaling ladders and siege towers to invade.

Winds of Change

Throughout the ages a good defense was bound to encourage an opponent to create more effective weaponry. This, in turn, spurred people to come up with better defensive tactics. While weapons were continually being perfected and fine-tuned over time, their basic form and function remained the same. The swords, spears, axes, and bows and arrows that were wielded by the Sumerian warrior at the dawn of civilization were still used in battle five thousand years later by the European knight. Many of these weapons were used around the world until the early twentieth century, though they would take a back seat to far more powerful arms.

By the early thirteenth century, however, change was on the horizon. Gunpowder was about to burst onto the scene. Weapons, warriors, and the world would never be the same.

An Explosive Discovery

Gunpowder is one of the world's most important innovations, yet we know little about its origins. No one knows who first discovered it, or where and when it happened. However, historical clues indicate gunpowder is likely from China, its discovery rooted in an ancient practice known as *alchemy.*

Based on the teachings of the Greek philosopher named Aristotle (384–322 B.C.), alchemy involved the study of matter.

Aristotle was an ancient Greek scientist and philosopher.

A miner holds gold nuggets in the palm of his hand. Ancient alchemists believed that more common metals such as iron and tin would naturally turn into gold over time. Today, we know that is not true.

Aristotle reasoned that all things in nature tended to strive for perfection. During the second century, artisans in Alexandria, Egypt, concluded that "less perfect" metals within the planet's crust sought to become "more perfect." They believed that, over time, common metals like iron, tin, and lead naturally transformed, or transmuted, into silver or gold. These scientists wondered if they could somehow copy nature and make gold themselves. Today, we know nature doesn't work this way, but at the time transmutation was an intriguing possibility. It popularized alchemy, the science of breaking down Earth's matter and recombining it to make new materials. The Catholic Church opposed alchemy. It would later object to dabbling with gunpowder, too, believing both to be inspired by the devil.

Vatican City is the seat of power of the Catholic Church. The church's leaders spoke out against the practice of alchemy.

Where There's Smoke . . .

While artisans in Egypt were trying to make gold, alchemists in the Far East were doing the same thing. Their interest in transmutation had more to do with health than with wealth. The Chinese believed gold was the key to prolonging life and, perhaps, living forever. Among the substances used by Chinese alchemists in early transmutation experiments were sulfer and saltpeter, also known as potassium nitrate. These are two of the three ingredients in gunpowder; the other is carbon in the form of charcoal.

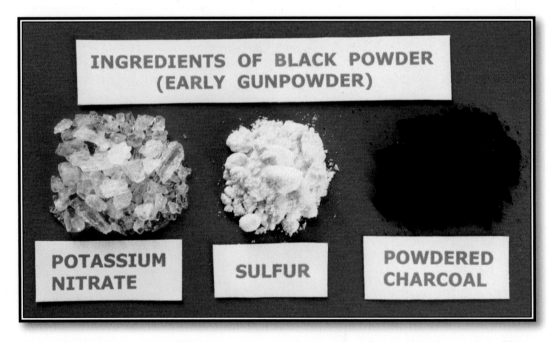

Two of the three ingredients in gunpowder—potassium nitrate and sulfur— were used by Chinese alchemists in some of their early transmutation experiments. Powdered charcoal is the third ingredient needed to make gunpowder.

Saltpeter is the main ingredient in gunpowder. It is created by bacteria feeding on decomposing human and animal waste products. It forms naturally in soil and can appear as a white, crusty buildup on rocks or walls. Saltpeter was once used like salt to bring out the flavor of food. Sulfur is a light yellow, tasteless, solid element that burns easily and gives off a smell similar to rotting eggs. Abundant in Earth's crust, it can be found around volcanoes and hot springs. Most of the planet's supply is located underground in gypsum and limestone. Charcoal is a black residue left behind after wood has been burned.

Behind the Boom

An explosive is any substance or device that, when ignited or detonated, produces rapidly expanding gases that exert extreme pressure. Here's how gunpowder works. When the substance is lit, the sulfur and carbon in the mix burn very fast. This fuel source draws oxygen from the saltpeter to continue burning. The fire produces hot gases that quickly expand. When the pressure of the expanding gases gets too great for the container, there is an explosion. If trapped in a closed container, the gases exert enough pressure to break it apart; that's called a bomb. If contained in an open tube, the gases are capable of blowing an object out of the tube (a gun) or propelling the tube itself into the air (a rocket).

An alchemist at work. The mixture that gave the world gunpowder was originally intended to be a drug to help people live longer.

Several centuries would pass before the earliest crude recipe for gunpowder was put on paper. It appeared in the book *Classified Essentials of the Mysterious Tao of the True Origin of Things,* written about 850. The author remains a mystery, yet his caution to others about avoiding huo yao, or the "fire drug," is clear:

Some have heated together sulfur, realgar [arsenic disulfide], and saltpeter with honey; smoke and flames result, so that their hands and faces have been burnt, and even the whole house where they were working burned down. Evidently, this only brings Taoism into discredit, and Taoist alchemists are thus warned clearly not to do it.

Alchemists originally intended a person to eat the thick, toffee like mixture to lengthen his or her life span. They had no idea that instead of making a brew to extend life, they were creating one that would take it. Where was the carbon in this recipe? It was in the honey. Carbon is the building block of all living things on Earth. It can be found in a variety of substances, from sugars to fuels. In making gunpowder, artisans would eventually come to prefer the carbon contained in charcoal.

About 1040, Tseng Kung-Liang, a Chinese government official, published the first true formula for gunpowder in a weaponry manual called *Collection of the Most Important Military Techniques.* In this manual, he gave several recipes for making bombs meant to be hurled by siege engines. The Chinese government, recognizing that gunpowder could be a powerful military tool, banned all exports of saltpeter and sulfur. But technology has a way of spreading. Over the next few hundred years, gunpowder was carried across Asia, through Arabia, and into Europe. In the thirteenth century, it fell into the hands of another alchemist, though this one had little interest in wealth or immortality. A pioneer in the field of science, his quest to unlock the secrets of gunpowder was fueled by a hunger for knowledge and truth. With the touch of a flame, he would discover both.

English philosopher and scientist Roger Bacon was born in about 1214 and died in 1292.

A True Scientist

In 1227, at just thirteen years old, Roger Bacon was already a student at England's Oxford University. He spent eight years there, excelling in nature studies, astronomy, mathematics, and philosophy. Deeply religious, Bacon also took vows to become a Franciscan monk. In the Catholic Church, however, a student was not supposed to question teachings that had been passed down through the generations. But Bacon was an independent thinker. He felt scientific theories should be tested, not simply accepted on blind faith.

Bacon found alchemy exciting. He knew that the Catholic Church considered it to be *heresy,* but the outspoken scientist was determined to research it. Historians don't know how Roger Bacon first acquired gunpowder. Perhaps a friend brought fireworks back from a trip to China. We do know that Bacon began experimenting with the mixture in a paper tube until a small explosion occurred.

Black Berthold: Man or Myth?

A statue in Freiburg, Germany, pays tribute to a fourteenth-century monk named Berthold Schwarz for discovering gunpowder and the cannon. Some historians say that while the man nicknamed Black Berthold (*schwarz* means "black" in German) may have experimented with gunpowder and early firearms, he certainly did not beat the Chinese or Roger Bacon in discovering the explosive. Other experts maintain that the German monk never existed at all, citing a lack of birth and death records. They say Black Berthold was purely a fairy tale created so Germans could lay claim to a discovery that played a key role in European history.

Fearing judgment from the church or perhaps concerned that gunpowder would fall into the wrong hands, Bacon wrote out his formula in an anagram, a type of code. In a letter titled On the Marvelous Power of Art and Nature, written about 1242, he wrote, "However, of saltpeter LURU VOPO VIR CAN UTRIET of sulfur; and with such a mixture you will produce a bright flash and a thundering noise, if you know the trick."

Bacon was also a Franciscan monk. Besides being the first person to detail the process of making gunpowder, he also imagined flying machines and motor driven carriages, inventions that were way ahead of his time.

Bacon's chance to air his personal views on scientific experimentation came in 1266, when Pope Clement IV invited him to submit his ideas. The pope thought Bacon had something already written. He didn't. Bacon quickly set to work and eventually filled three volumes with his musings on ways to study optics, physics, alchemy, and medicine. In the *Opus Tertium,* which means "third work," Roger Bacon details the deadly possibilities of gunpowder:

> When a quantity of the powder no bigger than a man's finger is wrapped up in a piece of parchment and ignited, it explodes with a blinding flash and a stunning noise. If a larger quantity were used, or if the case were made of some solid material, the explosion would of course be much more violent and the flash and din altogether unbearable.

One million words later, Bacon was ready to share his ideas with the world. Early in 1268, he sent his first two volumes, *Opus Majus (Great Work)* and *Opus Minus (Lesser Work),* to the pope. But it was too late. Pope Clement IV died before ever getting the chance to read Bacon's manuscripts.

Future church leaders would not be kind to Bacon. Believing him to be a heretic, Pope Nicholas IV had him arrested and jailed for ten years. Bacon died alone in a friary in Oxford, England, in 1292. Witnesses reported that his last words were, "I repent of having given myself so much trouble to destroy ignorance." In the two hundred years following his death, gossip and myth would reduce Roger Bacon to nothing more than a magician, the opposite of everything he stood for. Bacon's 840-page *Opus Majus* would not be published until 1733.

Clement IV was elected pope in 1265. He served as pope for fewer than four years. He died in 1268 before he had the chance to read Roger Bacon's manuscripts on the study of science.

Was Roger Bacon, with his vivid descriptions and secret code, warning future generations to stay away from gunpowder the same way a Chinese alchemist had done four hundred years before him? If so, it was advice that would be ignored. Gunpowder had cast its spell on humanity, and there was no turning back.

The Powder Makers

On New Year's Day 1800, a young Frenchman named Eleuthère Irénée du Pont de Nemours arrived in Newport, Rhode Island, with his father, older brother, and their families. The du Ponts had fled the turmoil of the French Revolution in search of a better life in the United States. Once in America, however, the family wasn't certain what kind of business to establish.

Eleuthère Irénée du Pont de Nemours founded E. I. du Pont de Nemours & Company in 1802. Still in business, the company he founded is now known as the DuPont Company.

E. I. du Pont sits at a table with Thomas Jefferson. The two men are discussing the location of du Pont's first gunpowder mill.

It wasn't long before Irénée, as he was known, had the answer. While out hunting, the twenty-nine-year-old had discovered that American-made gunpowder wasn't very good. Irénée, who had studied gunpowder production in France, was certain he could make better quality gunpowder. He convinced his father to let him try. After going back to France to raise money to buy the best machinery available, Irénée returned to the United States.

In 1802, he purchased a 235-acre (95-hectare) site along the Brandywine River near Wilmington, Delaware. Two years later, E. I. du Pont de Nemours & Company produced its first batch of *black powder.* It quickly gained a reputation for its superior quality. Within a decade, the company was the leading supplier of black powder to the U.S. government. Eventually, it would become the largest producer of gunpowder in the world.

Manufacturing gunpowder was not a safe task. Accidental explosions were a part of the job, and no gunpowder mill in the world was spared from disaster. All it took was one spark, set off by a speck of iron or an unprotected candle, and the whole works would blow. In its 118-year history, the E. I. du Pont de Nemours & Company gunpowder mill in Delaware had about three-hundred explosions that took 234 lives.

A Delicate Task

Gunpowder was first made using a pestle, a handheld tool with a rounded end, and a sturdy bowl called a mortar. In the fourteenth century, each of gunpowder's three dry, solid ingredients—saltpeter, sulfur, and charcoal—were ground separately before being incorporated, or mixed, to make a fine, black powder. It took one to two days to grind the powder properly. After the development of newer powders and manufacturing techniques, this mixture would become known as *serpentine.* It was based on the formula of 41.2 percent saltpeter and 29.4 percent each of sulfur and charcoal that Roger Bacon and others had outlined. Gunners usually mixed the serpentine themselves on the battlefield, because the powder could not be transported without the ingredients separating. Once its ingredients separated, the powder wouldn't ignite.

White Gold

Saltpeter, which forms on the waste products of humans and animals, is easily dissolved and washed away by rain. Originally, it was plentiful in places that had long, hot, dry seasons, such as China, North Africa, and India. Britain, with its wetter climate, wasn't as fortunate. The lack of saltpeter deposits in the United Kingdom lead the British government to take extraordinary steps to produce a substance that, in times of war, was more valuable than gold. In the thirteenth century, James I of Aragon gave "saltpeter men" the right to dig around barns for the white stuff to meet their weekly quotas. In 1625, King Charles I went so far as to order citizens to save their own urine and waste. By the mid-seventeenth century, many European nations, including England, were importing most of their saltpeter from India.

One hundred years later, powder makers were manufacturing serpentine in stamp mills. The raw materials were prepared and poured into a row of bowls hollowed out of an oak log. Powder makers also began adding a

Workers make gunpowder at an arsenal.

small amount of water to the mixture. They had discovered that a bit of clean water reduced the risk of explosion and helped the ingredients bond. The powder was incorporated using large, wooden pestles attached to springs or counterweights. Eventually, the pestles came to have copper feet because copper does not give off sparks when scratched. At first, the stamps were pumped by hand. By the middle of the fifteenth century, horse, water, and wind power took over. These early methods of making gunpowder were extremely dangerous. The dry ingredients often sent up a dust cloud that was easily ignited by a candle or flame. The United Kingdom outlawed most stamp mills in 1772. North America and France allowed powder makers to continue using them into the twentieth century.

Bigger, Better Bangs

The fifteenth century ushered in two important advances in gunpowder technology. First, there was a new recipe. Recognizing the quality and value of saltpeter in determining the force of an explosion (the more saltpeter, the bigger the blast), artisans had been gradually increasing the amount of saltpeter in the mix until the standard formula was 75 percent saltpeter, 15 percent charcoal, and 10 percent sulfur. These are the same proportions used in making black powder today. Second, powder makers added another step in processing gunpowder called corning.

Serpentine had its share of problems. The dusty powder took a while to burn and lacked power. It was so unreliable that, upon firing, it often exploded in a gunner's face. It also spoiled easily, not only because the ingredients tended to separate, but also because the powder was so fine, it often absorbed moisture right from the air. Once it is damp, black powder will not ignite. Corning solved all of these issues.

After the ingredients were ground together, they were moistened with water, vinegar, or urine and kneaded into 1-inch (2.5-centimeter) dumplings. A gunner would crumple the dumplings before loading them into a gun. Eventually, gunners pushed the dumplings through holes in a paper sieve. Tightly bonded within the corned granules, the ingredients were no longer apt to separate. They burned faster and more consistently. *Corned powder* was more powerful than serpentine and far less likely to be ruined by moisture.

By 1700, stamp mills in England were being replaced by wheel mills, also called pounding mills. In a wheel mill each major step in the manufacturing process was housed in a different building, so that if one section blew, it didn't take the whole works with it.

An illustration from a mid-fifteenth century German book shows a master gunner supervising workers pounding the mixture of ingredients into gunpowder.

Making Gunpowder in Wheel Mills

1. **Coal House:** *Controlled burning of trees harvested on-site*

2. **Refinery:** *Saltpeter and sulfur are refined separately; saltpeter is sent to the composition house, while sulfur is sent to the dust mill to be combined with charcoal.*

3. **Dust Mill:** *Sulfur and charcoal are pulverized into a ball to make "dust."*

4. **Composition House:** *Sulfur and charcoal dust is weighed and then mixed with saltpeter.*

5. **Roll Mill:** *Ingredients are incorporated under edge runners to make a wheel cake.*

6. **Press House:** *The wheel cake runs through wooden rollers, is pressed into slabs, and is broken up into smaller chips.*

7. **Corning Mill:** *Chips are made into grains and sorted by size.*

8. **Glaze Mill:** *Grains are polished in drums, coated with graphite, and dried.*

9. **Pack House:** *Powder is screened to remove fine particles and then packed in containers for transport.*

After the ingredients were refined and combined, the mixture was sent to the roll mill for incorporation. At the roll mill a pair of heavy wheels, called edge runners, rotated side by side over a bed to make what was called a wheel cake. At first the wheels and bed were made of stone, but later iron was used (the edge runners rode on top of the powder, so there was no danger of sparking). Each wheel was 5 to 6 feet (1.5 to 2 m) in diameter and weighed between 8 and 10 tons (7.3 to 9 metric tons). The edge runners were set in motion by a series of gears powered by a giant waterwheel. The bulk of explosions that occurred took place during this process. It was up to the workers to make sure the gunpowder stayed moist at all times. If the powder was too dry, it would send up a dust cloud that could easily ignite. If it was too wet, it would form into hard chunks called clinkers. An edge runner rolling over a clinker could cause the other edge runner on the same axle to break through the powder and hit the bed plate. The metal to metal contact could spark an explosion. Ordinary blasting powders took about an hour to grind, while high quality powders used for hunting took four or more hours.

After incorporation, the wheel cake was ready to go to the press house. Gunpowder was usually sent from one building to the next on a flatbed car. Workers would push the car down wooden sidewalks called duckboards. Later, steel rails would be used. In some British mills, small barges would float down a canal or waterway to move the powder between buildings.

At the press house, the powder was squeezed through wooden rollers and compacted into slabs. The pressing process tightly packed the powder and made it more powerful. The slabs were broken up into chips and then sent to the corning mill to be broken into grains and sorted.

The next stop was the glaze mill, where the corned grains were polished for several hours in a drum and glazed, or coated, with graphite. The last step was drying the powder. Originally, gunpowder was dried in ovens or on tables in the sun. By the end of the nineteenth century, it was dried inside the glaze barrels. For transport by barge, wagon, or train, gunpowder was packed into tin kegs or wooden barrels.

Wooden barrels, such as these at historic Fort Loudoun in Vonore, Tennessee, were used to transport gunpowder.

These mill buildings are part of the original DuPont gunpowder mill north of Wilmington, Delaware.

A Lasting Legacy

Because of the threat of explosion, gunpowder mills were always located far away from major cities. Being located on a river or a seaport was a must. Besides being essential for powering the mill's waterwheel, the port allowed

42

The American Colonies' Fight for Independence

In the eighteenth century, the American colonies imported nearly all of their gunpowder from Great Britain, a situation that became a grave concern prior to the American Revolution (1775–1783). In the fall of 1774, Great Britain stopped exporting gunpowder to the colonies, and the colonies scrambled to increase French imports and establish domestic mills. In the summer of 1775, only a few months into the Revolution, General George Washington wrote, "Our situation in the article of powder is much more alarming than I had the most distant idea of. We have but 32 barrels." In 1776, Benjamin Franklin was so worried about dwindling gunpowder supplies he suggested

issuing soldiers bows and arrows, calling them "good weapons, not wisely laid aside." Thankfully, things didn't get that bad. During the first years of the war, the colonies were able to import 1.5 million pounds (681,000 kg) of gunpowder. By the end of the conflict, the United States had set up more than twenty-five gunpowder mills, mainly in Pennsylvania, Massachusetts, Maryland, and Kentucky.

saltpeter and sulfur to be shipped in and the finished product to be shipped out. It was also necessary to situate the mill near an ample supply of willow, alder, hazelwood, and dogwood trees that could be burned to make charcoal.

The people who settled in a small, isolated mill town formed a tight-knit community. Frequently, workers lived in company-provided housing within walking distance of the mill. They were well paid and well treated, though the hours in the summer were dawn to dusk, and the safety regulations were strict. Each morning workers passed through a security checkpoint inside the gates. No jewelry, hair clips, or boots with metal nails were allowed. Cigarettes and matches were forbidden. When possible, relatives worked in separate buildings so that if an explosion happened, several members of the same family would not be killed.

Despite the safety precautions every gunpowder mill had its share of accidental explosions. Workers knew the risks they faced and willingly accepted them. They took pride in belonging to an elite group who, through commitment, craftsmanship, and courage, dared to do what others would not.

Ready, Aim, Fire!

Less than one hundred years after a Chinese alchemist warned of the "fire drug," China's military was making the deadly link between gunpowder and weaponry. In the tenth century, they introduced an artillery device called a fire-lance. Gunpowder was packed into a bamboo tube along with various items, including bits of pottery, iron chips, steel balls, stones, and human or

This fifteenth-century weapon was similar to a fire-lance.

animal waste. When ignited, the fire-lance showered its deadly and disgusting ammunition on enemy troops. It wasn't a true gun, however, because it didn't use projectiles specifically designed to fit its barrel.

Historians don't know who invented the first true gun, but evidence reveals that the Chinese were ahead of the game in weapons development. A 1-foot (30-cm), bronze gun that archaeologists date to 1288 was excavated at a site in Heilongjiang Province in northeastern China. The 8-pound (3.6-kg) gun was equipped with a small *touchhole* for igniting the powder and an enlarged barrel to keep the force of the explosion from splitting the weapon apart. The Chinese also produced some of the first military rockets, grenades, chemical bombs, and sea and land mines. These early Chinese breakthroughs in firearms technology in the thirteenth century would soon be overshadowed by European technical achievements in the centuries to follow.

Echoes of Gunpowder

In Europe, the earliest illustration of a gun appears in a manuscript written in 1326 called *On the Majesty, Wisdom and Prudence of Kings* by Walter de Milemete, chaplain to England's King Edward III. The manuscript, which discusses the duties of a king, includes a drawing of a soldier touching a hot rod to the vent of a pear-shaped cannon to fire a bolt. De Milemete, however, makes no reference to the gun in the text, so we don't know if it actually existed.

Crafted by bell makers, the first European cannons were fairly small and shot arrows or stones that were loaded from the muzzle, or front. By the end of the century, guns would also be loaded from the back, or breech. These early cannons were made of bronze, but by the 1370s, artisans be-

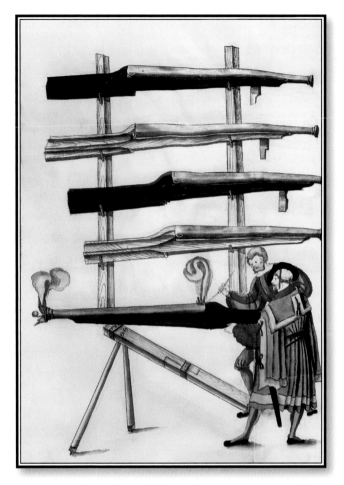

An arquebus is a fifteenth-century gun that was portable, but heavy. It was usually fired from a support.

gan to cast them from iron as well. They were crude cannons that didn't shoot very well or very far but, at the time, these shortcomings didn't matter.

By the latter half of the fourteenth century, European armies were beginning to realize that a stone or metal cannonball propelled by the force of gunpowder was far more effective at shattering a castle or city wall than catapults and trebuchets. As a result, artisans began making wrought-iron supercannons known as bombards. The term comes from the Greek word *bombos,* meaning "booming sound." These beasts measured 10 to 15 feet (3 to 4.6 m) in length, tipped the scales at 20 tons (18 metric tons) or (18 t) or more, and fired cannonballs weighing several hundred pounds. Now, instead of having to mount an endless, exhausting siege, an army could topple a nobleman's realm in a matter of weeks or even days.

Bombards (numbered 1 and 3) are shown along with other types of artillery one might have found on a battlefield a few hundred years ago.

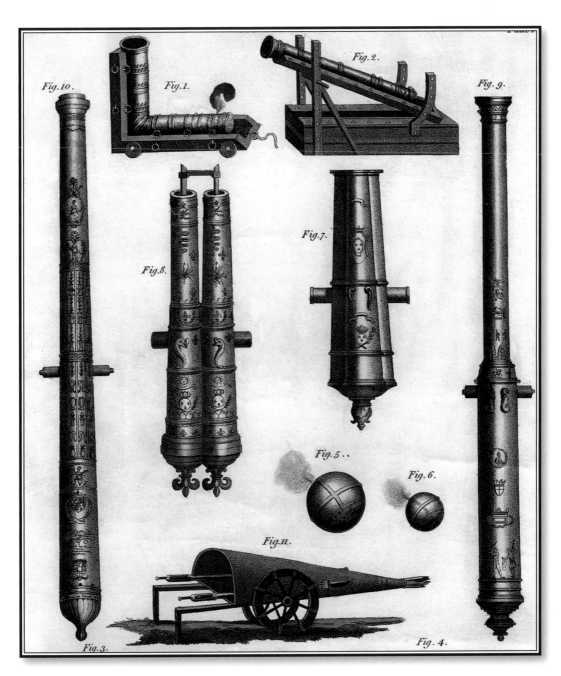

Over time, many different kinds of cannons and bombs were designed. This illustration from 1798 shows several of them.

"The Manual Exercise of the Foot Guards" is a pamphlet from the 1600s demonstrating how to load a musket. Six pictures from the pamphlet are shown here.

While some European cannons were getting larger, others were getting smaller. Soon, a new type of firearm would doom all the personal weapons that had come before it. After nearly five thousand years, the traditions of meeting a rival at close range for hand-to-hand combat and of displaying prowess with bow and sword were coming to an end.

In the Line of Fire

Developed in Germany during the fourteenth century, early European handguns were miniature cannons. The first "hand cannon" was a 4- to 8-inch (10- to 20-cm) metal barrel attached to a wooden stick. A gunner lit the gunpowder with a hot wire through a touchhole in the bottom of the gun while aiming it—a feat that was virtually impossible without help. These primitive guns fired slowly and inaccurately, sent up a lot of smoke, and, at best, shot a metal ball about 50 yards (46 m). They were so unreliable that the gunner was usually in more danger than the person he was trying to shoot. Like the cannon, early handguns, were most effective at frightening people and horses.

Over time, the barrel was lengthened to improve accuracy, curved stocks were added for bracing the gun against the shoulder, and a *flash pan* was added near the touchhole to ignite the main charge. New mechanical ways to light the powder were developed and fine-tuned to allow the gunner to keep both hands on the weapon. These improvements ushered in the age of the musket.

In use from the fifteenth to the nineteenth century, muskets were preferred by most militaries, though they were far from trouble-free. The gun had to be loaded from the muzzle, leaving the gunner open to enemy fire as he prepared to shoot. A soldier could get off only two or three shots per minute, if he was lucky enough to find a target through the thick clouds of smoke the guns produced. The musket was also terribly unreliable, firing only

Brown Bess is a nickname given to the muskets used by the British military during the American Revolution.

about half the time and rarely firing at all in the rain. Once again, accuracy was an issue. Brown Bess, a *flintlock musket,* was favored by the British military for more than 150 years even though it was so inaccurate it wasn't even fitted with a device for aiming known as a sight.

It took several hundred years for handguns to eclipse the accurate, dependable, rapid-firing longbow. Small arms caught on not because they were more effective than traditional weapons, but because they could be used by anyone. Muskets took only a week or two to learn to use, a breeze compared to the years required to master the sword or bow and arrow. Guns not only continued the trend begun by the longbow that allowed for killing from afar, but also inflicted greater wounds. Lead bullets tore through flesh, ripped apart internal organs, and caused infections so serious that stricken limbs frequently had to be amputated. Firearms were a source of power, and everyone, from citizen to criminal, peasant to prince, had access to them. The simple pull of a trigger was all that was needed to take down an enemy. "The real use of gunpowder," wrote nineteenth-century British author Thomas Carlyle, "is to make all men tall."

Though bows and arrows are seldom used in battle today, archery is an Olympic sport.

As the days of the European knight were fading, professional armies began to rise up, fan out, and conquer other civilizations. Beginning in the fifteenth century, countries such as Spain, Britain, France, and Portugal extended their reach by overwhelming native tribes of other lands. The bows and arrows, slings, spears, and swords of native peoples could not defend them against

Guy Fawkes is the most well-known member of the group that plotted to blow up the Parliament building and kill King James I and his ministers.

The Gunpowder Plot

In the early hours of November 5, 1605, an English soldier named Guy Fawkes was discovered by police in a storeroom under the Palace of Westminster. Just above the storage area, Great Britain's government, known as Parliament, was about to go into session. Thirty-six barrels of gunpowder lined the cellar, and Fawkes had a batch of fuses on him. He was arrested and taken to the Tower of London where, after a few days of torture, he confessed to being part of a plot to blow up the king and the House of Lords. The conspiracy was hatched by a group of Catholics who wanted to overthrow King James I for supporting anti-Catholic laws. After stashing 3,600 pounds (1,634 kg) of gunpowder in the cellar under the palace over the course of several months, Fawkes was to have lit the fuses the very morning he was caught. Government officials were tipped off to the plan by an anonymous letter. Fawkes and seven others were tried, found guilty, and hanged in a public execution. In the aftermath, life grew much worse for British Catholics. For years they were not allowed to get university degrees, practice law, serve in the military, or vote. Today, Guy Fawkes Day is celebrated in the United Kingdom on November 5 with bonfires, fireworks, and the following rhyme:

Please to remember the fifth of November
Gunpowder Treason and Plot
We know no reason why Gunpowder Treason
Should ever be forgot

European firepower. The Aztecs and Incas of South and Central America were defeated, as were the Maori of New Zealand and Aborigines of Australia. In time, native groups

55

around the world were overwhelmed by Western armies wielding gunpowder-propelled weapons.

Gunpowder had indeed made "all men tall," and it was only the beginning. Humans continued to seek and find better ways of delivering more firepower over longer distances. But the full story of gunpowder would not be limited to its impact on weaponry. In the eighteenth century, humanity came to realize that gunpowder was just as valuable—perhaps even more valuable—in times of peace as it was in war.

Like other native groups, American Indians with their bows and arrows were often defeated by the Europeans with guns.

CHAPTER SIX

Big Booms

At the onset of the nineteenth century, a growing population, plenty of land and resources, and many passionate inventors helped empower a new nation that had won its independence from British rule. To thrive as an industrial country, the United States had to tap into its natural resources like never before. It also needed to build a transportation system that could efficiently move supplies and goods. Gunpowder played a central role in accomplishing both tasks.

Foundation of a Nation

At one time, miners extracted Earth's ores by breaking rock with steel hammers, picks, chisels, and crowbars. A bonfire was lit next to the rock to heat it, then cold water

Fill 'Er Up with Gunpowder?

In 1673, Dutch scientist Christiaan Huygens described an engine he'd built as a "new motive power by means of gunpowder and the pressure of air." It involved using a small charge of gunpowder to push the air from the top of a cylinder through a one-way valve. When the hot gases cooled, the air pressure pushed a piston down. Huygens predicted that "motive power" could be used to operate mills, raise weights, and even fuel vehicles. Huygen's assistant, French physicist Denis Papin, constructed the engine but ran into several obstacles, one of which was finding a way to administer a continuous series of gunpowder charges to the cylinder. It is said that a better idea hit Papin as he watched steam lift the lid on a boiling teakettle. With that observation, gunpowder was out and water was in, giving rise to what would one day become the steam engine.

was thrown over it. This caused the rock to crack. Miners bored through the cracks and wedged the stone apart. This method was extremely slow and painstaking, and many times it didn't work.

In 1627, German engineer Kaspar Weindl demonstrated to Hungarian officials how gunpowder could do the job more efficiently. He packed gunpowder into a seam in rock, sealed it with a piece of wood, and ignited the powder. The resulting explosion fractured as much rock as it would have taken a crew of men a month to get through using hand tools. Impressive as this was, it took a while for gunpowder to catch on as a blasting tool. First, it took a lot of powder to break up a small section of rock, which made it an expensive way to mine. Also, miners were reluctant to use such a dangerous substance because there wasn't a safe way to light the powder. It grew in popularity, however, once more reliable fuses were developed.

Coal miners prepare an explosive charge in the 1860s.

In the United States, the nineteenth century brought staggering growth to the nation as millions of Europeans traveled across the Atlantic Ocean in search of land and jobs. Between 1790 and 1890, the U.S. population surged from 4 million to more than 60 million. By the middle of the

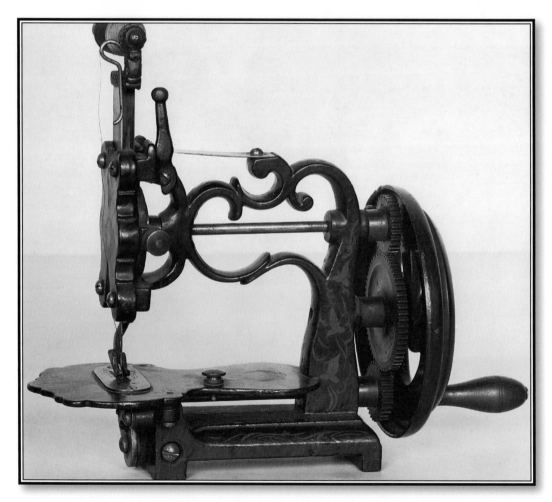

Iron and other metals were needed to keep up with the demand for sewing machines and other goods in the late 1700s and 1800s. Gunpowder was necessary to help mine the rocks and minerals.

Construction of the Erie Canal would have taken much longer if gunpowder had not been available to blast through rock and soil in the canal's path.

nineteenth century, U.S. gunpowder mills were cranking out 25 million tons (22.6 metric tons) of gunpowder per year. Some of it was required for weaponry, but much of it was used to mine the rocks and minerals necessary for the nation's blossoming economy. Coal was needed to power factories, drive steam engines, and heat homes. Copper was necessary for telegraph wires, electricity, and the telephone. Iron went into building heavy machinery and producing goods, such as plows, sewing machines, typewriters, and bicycles.

Workers had to blast their way through the Sierra Nevada's as they built the first transcontinental railroad.

Gunpowder was also vital to the growing transportation system. It blasted through rock, allowing workers to build roads, railways, tunnels, pipelines, and canals in a fraction of the time it would have taken to do the work by hand. So much of the explosive was needed for civil engineering work that gunpowder makers could barely keep up with demand.

In 1817, construction began on the Erie Canal, a 360-mile (579-km) waterway linking New York's Hudson River with Lake Erie. Completed eight years later, the canal served as a main transportation artery between the East and the western frontier. In 1865, work got underway on the transcontinental railroad connecting Sacramento, California, to Omaha, Nebraska. The entire 1,775-mile (2,856 km) track was built using little but hand tools and gunpowder.

In 1857, Lammot du Pont (Irénée's grandson) substituted sodium nitrate for the saltpeter (potassium nitrate) in gunpowder to create the first powder specifically meant for blasting. His special soda powder, dubbed "B," wasn't as good as traditional gunpowder, but it was far cheaper.

It was an instant hit and helped make DuPont a major player in the blasting industry.

The Industrial Revolution and the Civil War (1861–1865) kept American sales of gunpowder soaring through the 1860s. But the boom didn't last. Even as the du Ponts and other U.S. powder makers were enjoying their success, new, more powerful explosives were being developed. They would spell trouble for the future of gunpowder.

Christian Friedrich Schönbein was born in 1799 and died in 1868. Besides his discovery of nitrocellulose, he is also known for his discovery of ozone in 1840.

Oil workers fill a well shell with nitroglycerin. Created in 1846 by Italian chemist Ascanio Sobrero, early forms of this explosive were extremely dangerous to work with.

The Quest for More Power

In 1846, German chemist Christian Friedrich Schönbein accidentally discovered that dipping cotton (cellulose) into nitric and sulfuric acids made the fabric explosive. When ignited, *guncotton* (nitrocellulose) exploded with much more force than gunpowder, yet gave off virtually no smoke. Guncotton was a revolutionary find, but it was too unstable to use in weapons. In 1886, French chemistry professor Paul Vieille mixed nitrocellulose with other chemicals to make a safer, smokeless powder that would work in firearms and artillery. He called it "poudre B." As inventors raced to compete, other smokeless powders, such as cordite and *ballistite,* hit the market before the decade was out.

The advent of smokeless powders marked the beginning of the end for black powder (smokeless powders were light gray in color; to avoid confusion, the new powders were referred to as gunpowder, while the traditional formula became known as black powder). Smokeless powders could be made several times more powerful than black powder, yet left little residue in guns. Also, when a soldier fired his weapon, there was no thick cloud of white smoke to tip off the enemy to his position. Smokeless powders would make rapid-fire weapons, such as the repeating rifle and machine guns, a reality. In the twentieth century, they would be used to help launch missiles and space rockets and to fire up the engines quickly in fighter aircraft.

Nineteenth-century scientists found that combining other substances with nitric and sulfuric acids, a process called nitration, could produce different types of explosives. Soon, inventors gave the world *high explosives,* such as TNT (trinitrotoluene) and *nitroglycerin.*

A highly volatile liquid, nitroglycerin is eight times more powerful than gunpowder. However, it is extremely sensitive, often blowing up unexpectedly. It killed so many miners in the United States that the U.S. government outlawed its use in 1860. In 1867, Swedish chemist Alfred Nobel, who was one of the first

Alfred Nobel was born in Stockholm, Sweden, in 1833. When he died in 1896, his will required that most of his fortune be used to establish the Nobel Prizes. He wanted five awards given out each year "to those who, during the preceding year, shall have conferred the greatest benefit on mankind."

to manufacture and sell nitroglycerin, came up with a way to make the explosive safer to use. He mixed it with a type of porous clay that could be shaped into sticks. Miners could then drill holes into rock and insert the sticks for blasting. Nobel called his invention dynamite.

Tug of War and Peace

Alfred Nobel, owner of a gun factory and inventor of dynamite and ballistite, considered his work to be a contribution to the Industrial Age. Nobel felt the deadly substances he created only helped humanity realize the insanity of ever using them. He once wrote to a friend, "The day two armies have the capacity to annihilate each other within a few seconds, it is then likely that all civilized nations will turn their back on warfare." So Nobel was shocked when, in 1888, a French newspaper mistakenly printed his obituary instead of his brother's and referred to him as the "merchant of death." Haunted by the title, the Swedish chemist established a fund that, upon his death, honored those individuals who made outstanding strides in the areas of science, medicine, literature, and peace.

Between 1870 and 1910, more than twenty different kinds of high explosives were created. Smokeless powders had gradually replaced black powder in guns, but high explosives quickly elbowed their way into the areas of mining, quarrying, demolition, and civil engineering. As weapons advanced, high explosives came to be preferred over *low explosives* for use in mines, bombs, rockets, missiles, and torpedoes.

Following the Civil War, the surplus of black powder on the market caused problems for U.S. gunpowder makers. By the end of the century, the introduction of new and better explosives coupled with unfair trade practices of the Gunpowder Association forced most of the mills in the United States to close their doors. DuPont turned much of its attention to producing high explosives and products made from nitrocellulose processed with other chemicals. This created a non-explosive end product that was used for the manufacture of items such as film, corset stays, and shirt-collar stiffeners. They also branched out into paint, plastics, and fabrics, inventing such familiar products as nylon and Lycra. In 1921, after 117 years, the wheels stopped turning at Irénée du Pont's original gunpowder works along the Brandywine River. After more than eight hundred years, the glory days of gunpowder had come to an end.

Coming Around Again

Gunpowder's history is a mosaic of contradictions. On one hand, it spawned a new age of weaponry, allowing humans to destroy as never before. On the other hand, the nations of the world could not have industrialized without it.

Today, black powder is still manufactured in places

such as China, North America, and Switzerland. It's put to work in mining slate and quartz because it doesn't shatter rock the way high explosives do. Because of its slow, consistent burn rate, black powder is also used in fuses and as a primer for larger guns and cannons. It can be found in gun cartridges that shoot blanks, often fired by gun hobbyists demonstrating antique firearms and artillery.

Black powder's main function in the modern world is as an ingredient in fireworks. It seems fitting that gunpowder has come full circle to end where it began so many centuries ago—not to take life, but to celebrate it. And with each sizzle, crackle, and ka-boom that showers the darkness with tinsel-tipped rain, we joyfully do just that.

Black powder is used to launch fireworks and break the shells apart. Different minerals produce the colored sparks: copper makes blue, strontium gives off red, barium creates green, and sodium makes yellow.

Gunpowder: A Timeline

The Chinese text *Classified Essentials of the Mysterious Tao of the True Origin of Things* reveals the explosive power of gunpowder.
p. 24

British scientist Roger Bacon writes down his gunpowder formula in code.
p. 27

Gunpowder mills are established in the United States to make gunpowder for the American Revolution.
p. 43

| 850 | 900 | 1242 | 1627 | 1775 |

The Chinese invent fireworks, war rockets, and the fire-lance.
p. 5

German engineer Kaspar Weindl demonstrates the use of gunpowder to fracture rock and make mining easier.
p. 58

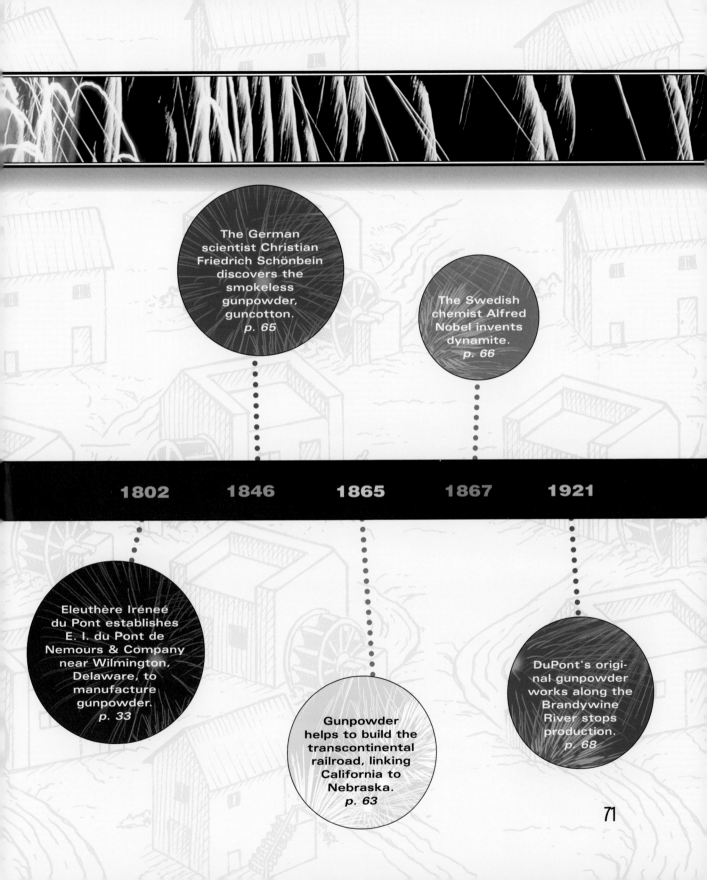

The German scientist Christian Friedrich Schönbein discovers the smokeless gunpowder, guncotton.
p. 65

The Swedish chemist Alfred Nobel invents dynamite.
p. 66

1802 **1846** **1865** **1867** **1921**

Eleuthère Iréneé du Pont establishes E. I. du Pont de Nemours & Company near Wilmington, Delaware, to manufacture gunpowder.
p. 33

Gunpowder helps to build the transcontinental railroad, linking California to Nebraska.
p. 63

DuPont's original gunpowder works along the Brandywine River stops production.
p. 68

Glossary

alchemy: the study of matter and the process of breaking down Earth's elements and recombining them

ammunition: sticks, stones, arrows, bullets, cannonballs, missiles, or other objects used as projectile weapons

artillery: military weapons, such as catapults, trebuchets, cannons, and tanks

ballistite: a type of smokeless powder containing guncotton, nitroglycerin, and other chemicals, invented by Alfred Nobel

black powder: a type of early gunpowder consisting of a mixture of saltpeter, sulfur, and charcoal

civil engineer: a trained professional who specializes in the planning, design, and construction of roads, dams, canals, and bridges

corned powder: gunpowder that was wetted and made into small grains that were stronger, more powerful, and more resistant to moisture than serpentine

flash pan: a small, saucerlike metal plate located near the touchhole of a gun that holds priming powder; when ignited, the powder in the pan lights the main charge of gunpowder to fire the weapon

flintlock musket: a type of musket that used a cocking mechanism containing flint

guncotton: an explosive material comprised of cotton (cellulose) and nitric and sulfuric acids from which smokeless gunpowders were derived; also called nitrocellulose

heresy: an opinion or doctrine that contradicts traditional religious teachings

high explosive: a liquid or solid substance that explodes with a force far surpassing the pressure of a low explosive; nitroglycerin, dynamite, and TNT are high explosives

low explosive: a slow-burning explosive, such as gunpowder

nitroglycerin: a clear, oily, highly explosive liquid eight times more powerful than gunpowder that is mixed with porous clay to make the more stable explosive dynamite

nomadic: relating to a lifestyle in which someone wanders from one place to another in search of food

propellant: a device or explosive that pushes an object forward; gunpowder propels a bullet or cannon from a gun

serpentine: an early form of black powder in which the ingredients were incorporated but not processed

shells: in fireworks, a circular-shaped paper casing propelled into the air, that contains black powder and stars

siege: a military operation whereby an army cuts off all access to a city or castle and may use weapons, starvation, and other tactics to force a surrender

stars: in fireworks, mineral pellets that are packed into shells and, upon explosion, create colorful sparks

touchhole: the opening near the breech in an early gun or cannon that allowed the gunner to ignite the gunpowder inside

To Find Out More

Books

Collier, James Lincoln. *Gunpowder and Weaponry.* New York, NY: Marshall Cavendish, 2003.

Woods, Michael & Mary B. *Woods. Ancient Warfare: From Clubs to Catapults.* Minneapolis, MN: Lerner Publishing Group, 2000.

Worth, Richard. *Gunpowder.* Philadelphia, PA: Chelsea House, 2003.

Videos

Fireworks, Windfall Films, NOVA/WGBH, 2002.

Kaboom! NOVA/WGBH, 1997.

The Story of the Gun, Volumes I, II, III & IV, A & E Home Video, 1999.

Web Sites

Fireworks!
NOVA ONLINE, PBS
www.pbs.org/wgbh/nova/fireworks
This website takes you inside the world of fireworks. Take a tour to find out how shells are made and how they work. You can also watch video clips of various types of fireworks bursting in air.

The Gunpowder Plot
www.bbc.co.uk/history/games/gunpowder/index.shtml
Log on to this British television network's Web site to learn more about the conspirators who attempted to overthrow a king. Find out what might have happened had their plan succeeded.

Organizations

Hagley Museum and Library
PO Box 3630
Wilmington, DE 19807-0630
(302) 658-2400
www.hagley.lib.de.us and *www.heritage.dupont.com*
The Hagley Museum is home to the original site of the E. I. du Pont de Nemours gunpowder works in Delaware. At both Web sites, you can read about the history of one of the world's most significant gunpowder mills and its founding family.

Index

About the Author

Trudi Strain Trueit is an award-winning broadcast journalist who has contributed news stories to ABC News, CBS News, and CNN. She now specializes in writing fiction and nonfiction for children and young adults.

In researching *Gunpowder,* Trueit spoke with several experts in the field of gunpowder history. In addition to conducting interviews and performing Internet research, Trueit read numerous books and articles on gunpowder, including Brian Cleggs's *The First Scientist: The Life of Roger Bacon* and *Oh Ye Had to Be Careful: Personal Recollections by Roslin Gunpowder Mill Factory Workers* by Ian MacDougall.

Born and raised in the Pacific Northwest, Trueit has a B.A. in broadcast journalism. She makes her home in Everett, Washington, with her husband, Bill.

DISCARD
Peabody Public Library
Columbia City, IN